Abstract

The paper examines Sea Basing with regard to operational functions of operational command and control, movement and maneuver, operational intelligence, surveillance, and reconnaissance, operational fires, operational logistics, and operational protection. The focus is on what Sea Basing could provide the combatant commander twenty years from now compared to what current carrier and expeditionary strike groups and maritime prepositioning force ships provide a combatant commander today.

The question of whether Sea Basing is really a transformational concept or simply the next logical step in the continuing development of amphibious warfare is discussed with an eye toward the potential capability tradeoffs faced by the combatant commander resulting from technology and cost tradeoffs.

When the Chief of Naval Operations, Admiral Clark, set forth his Sea Power 21 vision in 2002, he based it on three fundamental concepts: Sea Strike, Sea Shield, and Sea Basing[1]. The idea of Sea Basing is to enhance operational independence and support for the joint force. The vision laid out a plan where Sea Basing would enhance the joint commander's ability to take advantage of the vast maneuver space of the sea by providing enhanced afloat positioning of joint assets and providing offensive and defensive power projection. It would provide a commander with maneuverable, better protected command and control at sea, would integrate joint logistics, and would greatly accelerate deployment timelines[2].

The sea base is envisioned to be comprised of carrier strike groups (CSG), expeditionary strike groups (ESG), combat logistics force ships, maritime prepositioning force ships (MPF), and high speed support vessels[3]. This force would represent a "sovereign, maneuverable capability for assembling, equipping, supporting, and sustaining scalable forcible entry operations without the need for land bases in the joint area of operations"[4]. This paper will use the Defense Science Board assumption of a sea base that is sized to support operations for a Marine Expeditionary Brigade (MEB) size force of approximately 15,000 Marines[5].

Is the Sea Basing concept really transformational? Will Sea Basing revolutionize the way we fight? Many people would argue Sea Basing is not actually transformational, but that it does represent the next logical step in the progression of modern warfare. While not radically different from current Navy / Marine Corps operational capabilities and practices, Sea Basing can, in the end, provide a bigger, faster, more joint way of fighting. Sea Basing will take the best practices from how the Navy and Marine Corps have been training and operating for decades, and with help from advances in technology will develop a concept that will fulfill the needs of a combatant commander in the years to come.

This paper will look at what Sea Basing is planned to be, and what it should become. Future combatant commanders will need to know how they should employ Sea Basing. This will include understanding what additional capabilities Sea Basing brings them, what it does not bring them, what current capabilities will be enhanced, and what current capabilities might be diminished.

In this age of coalition building and with American bases spread around the world, it might seem America should be drawing down her naval and amphibious capability. The U.S. military already has shipping that can and often does deliver MEU size forces ashore around the world in response to a variety of events. These Marines are deployed around the world in ESG's on a continual basis. The ESG has sufficient organic air and sealift to deliver that force of 2,200 Marines to the beach. When the United States has a need to place a larger group of Marines or soldiers into a country, or to place them deeper into the country than the ESG is capable of doing, America works with a coalition of countries, including countries bordering the country of interest, to gain access to nearby air and sea ports of entry to allow the inflow of forces. This strategy has served America well in the past, but this may not always be the case. Some countries are reluctant to allow their sovereign territory to be used to attack a neighbor. The problem the American led coalition had in gaining permission from Turkey to enter northern Iraq through Turkish territory exemplifies the access problem. In that case a viable option existed and was used, but a future access problem might not be so easily overcome.

For example, suppose twenty years from now Tanzania was seen as a significant threat to the United States, but Kenya and Mozambique felt no threat from their neighbor and were unwilling to allow U.S. and coalition forces to base out of their countries. As the force is structured now, America and her partners would face a daunting task in getting enough combat power ashore quickly enough to fight effectively. While the threat of Tanzania is hypothetical, the access issue it highlights is real. Although individual ideas regarding what constitutes a vital national interest differ between people, it is safe to say that an underlying principle of all American administrations is that America shouldn't be prevented from acting in her own vital national interests due to access issues brought about by an inability to build a coalition of willing nations, and neighbors. This idea was stated by President Bush when he declared "While the United States will constantly strive to enlist the support of the international community, we will not hesitate to act alone, if necessary, to exercise our right of self-defense..."[6]. A combatant commander must have the capabilities necessary to implement the policies and objectives of the Commander in Chief. One of those capabilities includes the means to access foreign shores with a large enough force, from the sea if necessary, to carry out the will of the nation. The desire and stated intention to act alone in self-defense, far from U.S. borders could be easily ignored by an enemy if America were unable to act without first securing bases in a neighboring country.

The amphibious navy currently provides a limited forcible entry capability and the intent of Sea Basing is to enhance and expand that capability in the future. The Defense Science Board describes Sea Basing as a future capability with antecedents in amphibious operations[7]. The intent would be to bring war fighters, their material, command and control, operational fires, and a resupply capability together off the coast of a nation. From this sea base, American forces could then project power across the beach, and far deeper inland than current forces are capable of doing. Unlike an air or sea port in another country used by American forces to build up combat power prior to and during an operation, the sea base would represent sovereign U.S. territory. From this territory American forces would be able to project power without being affected by objections or political concerns from a third nation.

To understand the differences between Sea Basing of the future and amphibious operations of the present, with respect to employment by a combatant commander, it will help to compare and contrast them according to the operational functions of: provide operational command and control; provide operational intelligence, surveillance, and reconnaissance; conduct operational movement and maneuver; employ operational firepower; provide operational logistics and personnel support; and provide operational force protection [8].

Operational command and control is critical for success in any mission. Currently, a joint task force commander will generally set up in a neighboring country and run an operation from there, with the potential to move further forward when the situation allows. Some concepts of Sea Basing envision ships of the Maritime Prepositioning Force (Future) (MPF(F)) having not only large flight decks and a huge amount of storage space, but also a command-and-control center and accommodations for a joint force commander and their staff[9]. This would allow the joint force commander to command the operation from the sea. Command and control ashore is not a problem if there is secure ground space available near an operation for the commander, but as with

5

the earlier example, if the nearest option for a land based command-and-control center is a continent away, the ability to control an operation from the relative security of the sea while sitting twenty to a hundred miles off the coast would be extremely beneficial.

Limited deck space for antennas and concerns about interference between systems limits the bandwidth of today's ships. A land base will provide a joint task force commander more connectivity than will a ship. In spite of these problems, however, great improvements have been made over the past ten years. The Navy's aircraft carriers, large deck amphibious ships, and flagships have far greater connectivity and capability than did their predecessors. If the Sixth and Seventh Fleet Commanders can effectively command their forces from their flagships while at sea today, it does not seem a stretch to envision a more robust joint commander controlling operations from a ship ten or twenty years from now. The availability of a secure and effective command-and-control center at sea will greatly enhance the capabilities and options of a joint task force commander in the future.

The air, surface and subsurface assets available to a CSG or ESG today provide a fairly comprehensive Intelligence, Surveillance, and Reconnaissance (ISR) picture for the joint task force commander. In the future sea base, those same ISR assets can be combined with Army and Air Force assets to provide a much more robust picture. The Army's Training and Doctrine Command's Futures Center is actively exploring the potential for placing Army ISR assets on a sea base, without ever establishing a footprint ashore[10]. The ability to launch USAF or interagency UAV's from a sea base, with the downlink going directly to the joint task force commander on the sea base and also to the forces in the field will greatly benefit future operations. While UAV's generally have a fairly substantial loiter time, they often don't travel fast. This increases the importance of being able to launch the UAV's near where they will be used. In an operation today, if American forces were unable to launch ISR UAV's from a secure field in the country of interest or a neighboring country they would have to do without the information those UAV's could provide. The sea base could also serve as the point of origin for special operations forces to move in country to conduct surveillance operations. The idea of UAV's and SOF operating from sea is not new. In fact both have been done effectively in the past. What would be new would be the advanced capabilities and the joint and interagency nature of the operations, allowing the sea base of the future to provide American forces with greatly enhanced intel support and capabilities.

Movement and maneuver is another function that is essential to successful operations. Maneuver enables joint forces to gain positional advantage and to then achieve their operational objectives quickly and decisively[11]. According to joint doctrine, maneuver at the operational level is the "means by which the joint force commander sets the terms of battle by time and location, decline battle, or exploit existing situations"[12]. A sea base will allow the commander to take advantage of the vast maneuver room of the sea to move his forces to the best position from which to attack the enemy. Instead of being forced to attack a heavily defended port or airfield in order to gain a spot to bring in heavier forces, the joint commander will be able to send his forces to another location, bypassing the enemy's heavily defended sites, and even flying over them to locations further inland than is currently possible. Current doctrine calls for establishing a substantial logistics presence on the beach before a MEB moves inland[13]. In addition to the logistics and protection issues to be discussed later, this operational pause on the beach while forces are built up creates a "vulnerability gap"[14] that allows an enemy time to react to the landing, and to maneuver forces into position to delay or defeat the American forces before they reach full strength. The ability to more quickly insert and build up forces at a point of the combatant commander's choosing, further inland and less vulnerable to enemy counterattack than a fixed beachhead, will increase the combatant commander's flexibility and chance for success with the smallest number of casualties.

There is nothing new to the concept of using the vast sea to maneuver and attack where your enemy is not. The Athenians did it 2,500 years ago and militaries have been doing it ever since. The whole idea of forward deployed ESG's is that they allow a commander to have quick reaction forces readily available and can be moved around to attack where the enemy is not. The fact the ESG is limited to how far inland they can penetrate and how much heavy lift they can conduct is more a factor of currently available technology. The sea base will allow larger forces to attack from the sea, and will allow them to penetrate further inland with heavier forces and for a longer period of time than is currently possible, but this is not transformational. It is simply taking the maneuver capability of today's ESG and CSG and moving to the next logical step in the progression of modern warfare by developing and taking advantage of new technologies to become better, stronger, faster, and more joint.

A sea base will employ operational fires in much the same manner as today's ESG and CSG, only in a more advanced manner. The concept is that the sea base will include the forces of the ESG and CSG, so strike aircraft and land attack missiles will still be available to the joint commander. Naval gunfire today is relatively short range and not of much use to forces once they move away from the beach. Advances in naval gunfire will add to the fires capability of the sea base as the escort ships will have far greater ability to support the forces placed ashore far beyond the current range of naval guns. Added to these capabilities will be the joint forces of the sea base. A joint commander would be able to conduct a sizable operation in one location to deceive and tie down enemy forces while still being able to dedicate a substantial force to the real objective.

The biggest difference the joint commander will see with regard to the sea base is in the area of focused operational logistics. Focused logistics is "the ability to provide the joint force the right personnel, equipment, and supplies in the right place, at the right time, and in the right quantity, to support operational objectives"[15]. The sea base will provide the joint commander with a logistic hub at sea. The commander will be able to develop and sustain a large scale operation ashore without first having to take and defend an air or sea port. The ability to move the required equipment ashore, directly from the sea base to the forward forces without first building up a pile of equipment ashore will improve the speed and capability of the fighting forces. The principles of logistics, which include responsiveness, sustainability, survivability, and flexibility[16] will all be met by the sea base. The sea base is envisioned to serve as the logistics hub for a joint operation. Ships such as the MPF(F) will have the capability to reconfigure their loads at sea and selectively offload only the equipment required by the forces ashore. In the past forces had to secure a deep water port so these ships could pull pierside and offload their entire cargo. By keeping his logistics hub at sea and moving around or over an unsecured port the future commander will have a flexible, more survivable logistics hub.

Avoiding the pile of gear at a fixed, more vulnerable point ashore is perhaps the most transformational aspect of the sea base. Logistics to support the joint force however, also provides some of the key issues yet to be resolved with regard to Sea Basing. If the joint logistics piece can be worked out, the joint commander will need to consider another, equally important principle of logistics – reliability[17]. The Navy is looking seriously at selective offload, which is sending in what is needed, when it is needed, and where it is needed in order to avoid building the traditional "iron mountain" ashore[18]. This concept of just-in-time delivery has its background in the business world. The concern of the joint force commander if his forces are conducting just-in-time delivery is what happens to his war fighters at the tip of the spear if his delivery system fails for even a short period of time, whether due to enemy action, weather, equipment malfunctions, or some other problem. The initial idea would be to put extra gear ashore, but the question then becomes how much safety reserve is required, and at what level of safety reserve you defeat the intent of a sea based logistics hub.

Another logistics issue facing the combatant commander is the manner in which supplies and personnel will be brought from the rear area or CONUS to the sea base, and then from the sea base to the forces ashore. There are numerous concepts at this point. To get the personnel and gear from the rear area to the sea base large container ships could conduct skin to skin transfer of material to the sea base, a significant number of long range, heavy/vertical lift aircraft could be developed, or the sea base could be made large enough to accommodate existing heavy lift fixed wing aircraft. Once sorted, the next challenge becomes getting the personnel and gear from the sea base to the troops ashore. One concept includes developing heavy lift tilt rotor aircraft, similar to the

MV-22. Another idea would be to use high speed craft (HSC). Many, but not all, of the HSC being considered would still need to go pierside, although the offload time would be much shorter and their shallow draft would greatly increase the number of ports they could utilize.

The final operational function is operational protection. The sea base will provide the forces of the joint force commander a greater amount of force protection. While ships at sea are not invulnerable to threats, their ability to continually change their location and remain over the horizon, out of sight of land based enemy forces provide a key advantage over the iron mountain of forces and equipment ashore. In addition to the increased force protection provided by moving logistics out to sea, it would also free up ground soldiers who would otherwise be required to provide security for the land based logistics hub. While the cost of the ships required for protection of the sea base won't necessarily provide a net dollar savings, it does free up ground combatants, while shifting the commander's operational protection of the logistics hub to surface combatants already on hand. As technology advances, static positions ashore and enormous ships ponderously offloading supplies pier side at fixed GPS positions are increasingly vulnerable to attack from special forces, massed troops, missiles, artillery, and even weapons of mass destruction. One way to look at this problem is to consider the possibility of North Korea moving south and occupying a portion of South Korean territory. American forces would need to get reinforcing troops and equipment ashore, much of it presumably through deep water ports such as Pusan. It seems likely that after more than 50 years of study, the North Korean forces would have a fair number of missiles and a large amount of artillery focused on ports such as Pusan or Inchon. By moving the main base of operations offshore, and giving the joint task force commander the ability to go ashore in less predictable locations the commander significantly improves the operational protection posture of his or her forces.

As with other operational functions explored earlier, the concept of increased force protection offered to ships at sea as opposed to fixed sites ashore is not a new idea. What will be new is the technology that allows the sea base to move from the conceptual stage to a reality. The ability of the joint task force commander to have the bulk of his forces bypass the littorals; and the mines, small craft, and shore based missiles associated with that region will dramatically improve the commander's force protection outlook.

While the new capabilities of Sea Basing seem extremely beneficial, although not transformational, there are certain problems that will affect the ability of the joint task force commander to utilize this system to its full potential. These problems include cost, technology, and jointness.

As always, cost plays a major role in the decisions being made with regard to Sea Basing. Although the combatant commander is not specifically concerned with the development cost of any specific system, he or she does need to be concerned when the cost of a system results in the loss of a different, required capability. Joint Vision 2020 calls on leaders to "assess the efficacy of new ideas, the potential drawbacks to new concepts, the capabilities of potential adversaries, the costs versus benefits of new technologies, and the organizational implications of new capabilities"[19]. A November 2004 study by the Congressional Budget Office examined the Navy's plan to build and modernize the amphibious and maritime prepositioning force fleet over the next 30 years. The study determined the annual ship construction cost over the next 30 years (in 2005 dollars) necessary to support the Sea Basing concept would be double what has been spent annually over the last 25 years[20]. In fact, despite a 4.8 percent increase in overall defense spending for 2006, to $419 billion, the Navy has scaled back plans for new warships and submarines[21].

If the Navy has to cut its annual ship buy from six to four[22] in this time of expanding defense budgets it does not seem likely the Navy will be able to fully pursue its ambitious Sea Basing program while also maintaining the same level of cruiser, destroyer, and amphibious shipping currently on hand. While the Navy is looking at alternative ship types to include catamaran hulls and relatively inexpensive littoral combat ships, and programs such as Sea Swap to expand the forward presence capability of the Fleet, none of those initiatives are close to being fully developed.

This is where the issue of opportunity cost comes into play, and opportunity cost, while dealt with in Washington DC, will be felt by the combatant commander forward deployed. Opportunity cost is the value of the next best option not taken. In the situation described above, if the Navy normally spends $1 billion per year to build amphibious platforms, then Sea Basing done right would require doubling that amount to $2 billion. If there is a finite amount of money available for shipbuilding, however, and the budget cannot simply be doubled, then the extra $1 billion per year needed to build Sea Basing would have to come out of the current shipbuilding budget. The opportunity cost, therefore, is more than likely the cancellation of the amphibious ship construction or perhaps the cancellation of a cruiser instead.

What does the loss of some cruisers, destroyers, or amphibious ships mean to the combatant commander? Trading a cruiser or destroyer for every billion dollars spent on

Sea Basing means an erosion in the ability of the Navy to provide protection to the sea base from air, surface, and subsurface threats. Without its full screen of surface ships and submarines the sea base would be increasingly vulnerable to attack. Even at a hundred miles offshore the sea base could be threatened by enemy submarines, small ships, and land based aircraft. The British learned this lesson during the Falklands campaign, when their lack of a sufficient number of escort ships with the proper sensors left their logistics extremely vulnerable to attack. If the commander is unable to provide operational force protection for his sea base, the operational ISR, command and control, and logistics afforded by the sea base will be in jeopardy.

If the argument for maintaining the size of the escort fleet is strong enough, then the next place to make up the cost of the sea base is by cutting amphibious shipping. Amphibious ships represent a significant immediate response capability for the combatant commander. They are always forward deployed as part of an ESG, with 2,200 Marines embarked with the MEU(SOC). The ESG can respond on extremely short notice, and in the 1990's they took part in at least 55 crisis-response actions on behalf of the combatant commander[23]. Although the force coming off an ESG is smaller and less joint, and does not have the logistical capability or inland reach envisioned for the sea base (but not yet technologically feasible) the ESG still provides smaller scale operational maneuver, fire support, and force protection. Although the Navy is exploring different ideas and programs to get more forward deployed time from each ship, those efforts are still in the early stages. The Department of the Navy needs to ensure it does not lessen the ability of the combatant commander to respond on short notice to small scale crises over the next two decades while pursuing "a rich man's approach to solving the [larger scale] access denial problem"[24].

There are many issues that have not yet been finalized and technologies that have not yet been developed. Some possible platforms for Sea Basing include MPF(F), a Mobile Offshore Base (MOB), and a semi-submersible structure[25]. All of these platforms require the development of new and costly technologies. The vast quantity of material that must be moved to and through the sea base is a big sticking point. Large ships do not have the ability to transfer large containers between two ships at sea, and to do so by vertical lift would require an excessive number of aircraft. To move the equipment and supplies to the troops ashore from the sea base would require an even greater number of aircraft. To move the equipment ashore via high speed vessels is being considered, but those vessels require port facilities which would, to a degree, defeat the whole purpose of the sea base. Traditional landing craft can move the equipment ashore, but they are either too slow (LCU) or cannot carry enough cargo (LCAC) to make such a large operation feasible. One of the essential qualities of the sea base and the MPF(F) discussed previously is that the ships must be able to be selectively offloaded. In theory, if the forces ashore need what is stored in the bottom container on the ship, the logisticians must be able to get to that container and get it off the ship. This requires a shipboard container moving system which does not yet exist. In addition, the ability to move containers around on a ship would require a certain percentage of empty space to facilitate movement. This excess space will also add to the cost of the platform. The MOB and semi-submersible structure are extremely expensive and untested and might be too difficult to develop and will not be considered here. Another possibility is to take large fast ships, such as decommissioned or soon to be decommissioned aircraft carriers and convert them to sea base style ships. While they certainly have the necessary speed, their power plants are extremely manpower intensive and are probably not the best option.

Last is the issue of ensuring Sea Basing is fully joint. As discussed previously, there is initial buy-in to look at the possibilities on the part of the Army and Air Force. If the resultant system is not fully integrated and does not provide the Army and Air Force with required capabilities, they will be unable to fully utilize the system. In such a scenario, the commander will not have a system capable of supporting joint operations deep behind enemy lines with no requirement to establish a footprint ashore in a port facility. He or she will instead have a larger version of the MEU they currently possess. The same is true if the only ones working from the sea base are the Navy and Marine Corps. The United States already possesses the capability to work two MEBs from sea, and jumping the shoreline, but leaving other services out of the fight will not solve any problems.

An operational commander already has the ability to use an ESG and its Marines to strike from the sea on short notice. The commander already has the ability to deploy in excess of two MEB size forces from the sea on currently available amphibious shipping, although with a longer build up time, and with substantial resupply after the initial assault coming into sea ports on MPF shipping. The commander also has the ability to place a number of Army air assault forces, or special operations forces and their aircraft and equipment on a big deck amphib or aircraft carrier and operationally maneuver those forces via the sea prior to putting them ashore. What the commander needs, when air and sea ports are not available, is the ability to assemble, equip, support, and sustain a substantial joint force without the need for land bases in the joint area of operations.

In achieving this capability, however, the military cannot afford to remove other critical war fighting capabilities from the joint commander as a result of spending limitations. While this step forward is necessary to ensure the combatant commander of the future is able to fully exploit the situation and take the fight to the enemy, the Navy and the Department of Defense need to look at all possibilities, not just the largest and most costly options.

Exhausting the national treasury to build speedy, gigantic ships that don't provide any real new capability is a waste of valuable resources and is not transformational. Transformation is doing something differently and adding speed and range is not different. If the Navy doesn't actually do anything different then in the end they cannot expect anything to be different. If the technology does not exist and cannot be developed at an acceptable cost that doesn't strip other vital operational requirements, and if the Sea Basing system is not developed from the keel up as a fully joint system with full joint cooperation and agreement, then instead of being a force multiplier, Sea Basing will add nothing new to the arsenal of the operational commander. The Navy should not rush to develop Sea Basing simply to fulfill a vision full of concepts but without much understanding or agreement of how it will work. The concept is certainly worth pursuing, but the essential technologies and joint issues need to be ironed out. Ships are long term investments and the Navy should not commit billions of dollars to the effort with the hope of figuring things out along the way. A well thought out sea base that could support Marines, Army, and Special Operations Forces would prove extremely useful to a combatant commander. Sea Basing would provide a measured response capability with minimal staging requirements to trouble spots around the world, without the current requirement to offload all the gear ashore before moving inland. If the details don't get worked out though, Sea Basing will not provide the combatant commander with any new capabilities. It could actually rob the combatant commander of other essential capabilities they already possess, and ultimately weaken future operations.

[1] Admiral Vern Clark, "Sea Power 21 Projecting Decisive Joint Capabilities," U.S. Naval Institute Proceedings (October 2002): 33.

[2] Ibid., 36-37.

[3] Vice Admiral Charles W. Moore and Lieutenant General Edward Hanlon Jr., "Sea Basing Operational Independence for a New Century," U.S. Naval Institute Proceedings (January 2003): 81.

[4] Defense Science Board, "Defense Science Board Task Force on Sea Basing," Office of the Under Secretary of Defense for Acquisition, Technology, and Logistics (August 2003): 12.

[5] Ibid,. 13.

[6] President, "National Security Strategy of the United States of America," (September 2002): 6.

[7] Defense Science Board, 12.

[8] Joint Chiefs of Staff, Universal Joint Task List, CJCSM 3500.04C (Washington DC: 1 July 2002), appendix D.

[9] Richard C. Barnard, "Sea Basing Concept Promises a Revolution in Power Projection," Sea Power (June 2004): 12.

[10] Roxana Tiron, "Sea Base Hurdles: Deployment of Sea Bases Faces Technical, Budgetary Challenges," National Defense (January 2005): 30-32.

[11] Joint Chiefs of Staff, Joint Vision 2020 (Washington DC: June 2000), 20.

[12] Joint Chiefs of Staff, Doctrine for Joint Operations, Joint Pub 3-0 (Washington DC: 10 September 2001), IV-10.

[13] Defense Science Board, 16.

[14] Ibid., 29.

[15] Joint Chiefs of Staff, Joint Vision 2020, 24.

[16] Joint Chiefs of Staff, Doctrine for Logistic Support of Joint Operations, Joint Pub 4-0 (Washington DC: 6 April 2000), II-1 – II-3.

[17] Ibid.

[18] Hunter C. Keeter, "Interview with RADM John Kelly: Sea Basing Presents Infinite Number of Problems for the Enemy," Sea Power (June 2004): 24.

[19] Joint Chiefs of Staff, Joint Vision 2020, 11.

[20] "CBO Suggests Alternatives for Navy Sea Basing Plan" Aerospace Daily & Defense Report, 17 (November 2004): 5.

[21] Bryan Bender, "Navy To Cut Orders; Job Losses Seen," Boston Globe, 7 February 2005, sec A, p. 1.

[22] Tony Capaccio, "Bush Asks $419 Billion For Defense In 2006 Budget." Lkd. <u>DOD Early Bird</u>. <<u>http://www.bloomberg.com</u>> (3 February 2005).

[23] Christopher P. Cavas, "Sea Basing Would Cost Too Much, Budget Office Says," Navy Times, 06 (December 2004): 21.

[24] Ronald O'Rourke, Navy-Marine Corps Amphibious and Maritime Prepositioning Ship Programs: Background and Oversight Issues for Congress," Congressional Research Service Report for Congress (15 November 2004): 15.

[25] Defense Science Board, 69.

BIBLIOGRAPHY

Barnard, Richard C. "Sea Basing Concept Promises a Revolution in Power Projection." Sea Power (June 2004): 10-12.

_____. "Success of Sea Basing Concept Hinges on Effective Logistics Management Systems." Sea Power (June 2004): 20-21.

Cahlink, George. "Navy Eyes New Kinds of "Connectors" Between Sea Bases, Forces Ashore." Sea Power (June 2004): 18-19.

Cavas, Christopher P. "Sea Basing Would Cost Too Much, Budget Office Says." Navy Times, 06 (December 2004): 21.

Clark, Admiral Vern. "Sea Power 21, Projecting Decisive Joint Capabilities." U.S. Naval Institute Proceedings (October 2002): 32-41.

Corbett, Art and Vince Goulding. "Sea Basing: What's New?" U.S. Naval Institute Proceedings (November 2002): 34-39.

Gray, Captain Richard D. NWDC Logistics Doctrine (N54), Navy Warfare Development Command, interview by author, 08 February 2005, Newport, RI.

Keeter, Hunter C. "Interview with RADM John Kelly: Sea Basing Presents "Infinite Number of Problems" for the Enemy." Sea Power (June 2004): 22-24.

_____. Navy, Marine Corps Sea Base Effort Inspires Joint-Service Cooperation." Sea Power (June 2004): 14-16.

Klein, John J. and Rich Morales. "Sea Basing Isn't Just About the Sea." U.S. Naval Institute Proceedings (January 2004): 32-35.

Moore, Vice Admiral Charles Jr. and Lieutenant General Edward Hanlon Jr. "Sea Basing, Operational Independence for a New Century." U.S. Naval Institute Proceedings (January 2003): 80-85.

Office of the Under Secretary of Defense For Acquisition, Technology, and Logistics, Defense Science Board, Defense Science Board Task Force on Sea Basing. Washington, DC: August 2003.

O'Rourke, Ronald. "Navy-Marine Corps Amphibious and Maritime Prepositioning Ship Programs: Background and Oversight Issues for Congress." Congressional Research Service Report for Congress. 15 November 2004.

Peveler, David L. Coordinator, Sea Base Warfare Innovation Development Team, Navy Warfare Development Command, interview by author, 28 January 2005, Newport, RI.

Tiron, Roxana. "Sea Base Hurdles: Deployment of Sea Bases Faces Technical, Budgetary Challenges." National Defense, (January 2005): 30-32.

U.S. Department of Defense. Seabasing, Joint Integrating Concept – Draft Copy. Washington D.C.: 28 October 2004.

U.S. Joint Chiefs of Staff. Doctrine for Joint Operations. Joint Pub 3-0. Washington DC: 10 September 2001.

_____. Doctrine for Logistic Support of Joint Operations. Joint Pub 4-0. Washington DC: 6 April 2000.

_____. Joint Vision 2020. Washington DC (June 2000).

_____. Universal Joint Task List. CJCSM 3500.04C. Washington DC: 1 July 2002.

U.S. President. National Security Strategy of the United States of America. September 2002.